Dear Mom, It's Me... I Miss You!!!!!

By: Ashley Kammeraad Zuidema

ISBN: 978-1-960136-63-3

Acknowledgments

Ashley Kammeraad Zuidema, is a new, upcoming author. She is a collaborator in "The Mindful Journey" anthology and has a published article in Being an Unstoppable Woman Magazine. She lives in Zeeland, MI with her family. Ashley would like to thank her husband for his unending support in her writing, her family for assisting her with pertinent information in the process of this writing, and her editor for all of their continued support and assistance.

Dedication(s)

This book is dedicated to all the Daughters out there who have lost a loved one to cancer. Although the loss is never forgotten, remember you are not alone!

In Loving Memory of Pamula (Mulla) Kay Kammeraad
March 3, 1954 - April 4, 2004

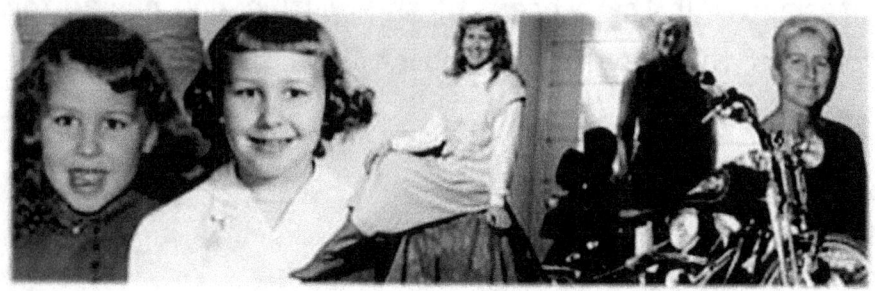

"She exists now... Only in my memories"
"Kate Winslet"

Background

Cancer is one of the hardest illnesses on an individual. Chemotherapy alone is enough to destroy the working functions of the body. Depending on the form and location of the Cancer, different treatment forms could be used. According to the American Cancer Society Journal, as of June 2014, Pancreatic Cancer is one of the most lethal cancers worldwide. No effective screening methods exist. To this day, pancreatic cancer is projected to be one of the leading causes of death in cancer patients.

On September 26, 2003, my mother was diagnosed with pancreatic and liver cancer. She was determined to fight it but sadly lost her battle on April 4, 2004. Within the Seven months, she lived her life the best she could. She went from a young vibrant woman to a skeleton wrapped in skin. Her eyes were sunken, very thin face, she had lost all of her hair, and had a bloated belly from the chemotherapy. This image of her will be forever burned into my mind. There are so many things that are really hard to let go of. When I saw her like that, it was way more than a twenty-year-old to handle.

According to the National Cancer Institute, the death rate of pancreatic cancer patients for every 100,000 men/women there were 11.1% that had died due to this illness. The percentage continues to increase year by year.

In the Beginning
1994 - 2004

Chapter 1

Dear Mom, It's Me...

What's wrong with Grandpa? Why is he in the hospital? What do you mean he is sick.? What happened to him? Is this why Dad is so sad? When can we go see him?

Cancer? What's cancer?

As you began to tell me what was wrong with Grandpa, I began to cry! I knew he was a smoker, but had no idea what it could do. You told me it was in his lungs and that he was very sick. You wanted to make sure that we understood that the tubes, wires, and machines were an effort to save his life.

It was dark outside as we headed to the hospital; we had been driving for a while. I could only assume that we were going to the Grand Rapids hospital. I couldn't be sure. Once we arrived, we parked and started to walk in. My stomach was in knots. I was nervous and scared at the same time. I didn't know what to think. It is hard to feel anything when you are unsure what's happening.

Once we got up to his room, I started to notice

everything that my mom was talking about. I had never seen my grandfather like this. He was sleeping comfortably in the hospital bed. With every beep of the machine, he slowly breathed in and out.

I had a feeling that would be the last time I got a chance to see him. I did not want to wake him up. I sat silently next to him, just looking.

We sat in silence for a while. Before I realized it, I was brought back to reality. When Dad said it was time to go, I slowly walked towards the door. I turned and looked at my grandfather for the last time.

He died a couple of hours later...

I Miss You!

Love,
Ashley

In Loving Memory of:
Herbert Jay Kammeraad
1922-1994
U.S. Army Veteran

Dear Mom, It's Me...

Today was Grandpa's funeral. It was sad, but really nice. It was no surprise how many people were there. Grandpa was popular and knew a lot of people. His army buddies who were still alive, were also there.

We were at the Pilgrim Home Cemetery. The service was next to the plot where Grandma is buried. It is nice to know they are back together, in Heaven. Even though Grandpa was happy to be with his partner, it was not the same. The entire family was sitting up front. They even allowed his partner to sit up front with us. I thought that was nice.

Once the pastor finished with his sermon, the uniformed representatives of the Veteran's service came over. Without even having to think about it, the four of them grabbed a corner of the United States of America flag. First, they folded it in half. Then, they folded it in half again. Lastly, they began to fold it from corner to corner. When they were done it looked like a triangle. The four of them began to walk over with the flag and handed it to Auntie (younger sister).

We sat in silence for a few minutes and then it came... the loud shatter of the guns. They shot in the air 21 times. It was very emotional for everyone at this point. I could tell you and Dad were sad. We proceeded to leave. There was a lunch at the church. At that point I was tired and my head hurt from crying so much. Not to mention my feet were hurting too.

Once we arrived at the church, it seemed like there were a lot more people. I guess I didn't really notice all of the people behind me. After, we ate and talked before everyone headed to Grandpa's house. It seemed empty without him there. I am going to miss him very much.

The whole family was there and then some. We decided to go back to the house for a while. We sat around in the living room and reminisced about all the times we had spent there. So many good times. I find it hard to believe that this form of family gathering will continue again in this capacity.

I Miss You!

Love,
Ashley

Dear Mom, It's Me…

Do you remember Christmas at Grandpa's house? The house was always warm and cozy. Everyone always came on Christmas Eve. I remember the roads to get there were always awful. Being out in the countryside, the snow was horrible. I was always so scared when we were driving here.

I remember once all the kids went to bed, (or so you thought) we would always sneak up to the top of the stairs and watch the grown-ups still wrapping presents. Some of us would figure out who was getting what. Yet, some of us still had no clue.

The tree was beautiful. I remember Grandpa always got a real tree. The lights and ornaments on it were prepossessing. Oh, and the presents, boy were the presents plentiful. Every year it seemed like the presents grew and grew in number. It always seemed like the presents overran the tree. It was so exciting to see what everyone got. It was even more entertaining to see what Christmas pranks everyone played on one another.

My little cousin would be up at the crack of dawn and running through the house saying "Santa came, Santa came!" I always wished that someone would teach that kid what a snooze button was. Not to mention Antie K snoring in her bed. Wow, could that women snore.

It was, without fail, an amazing time. This holiday at Grandpa's will be the one that I miss the most. I loved how the family always spent time together on this beautiful property. I always dreamed that I would get married out there. Setting up the altar by the barn, coming down the stone steps in my wedding gown, having a red carpet through the grass, and using the second driveway as a means to drive out with the limo. I do not think that this will happen now. I am sure that the family is going to try to sell the property. There is no way a new owner will allow me to live out my dreams. Oh well.

I Miss You!

Love,
Ashley

Dear Mom, It's Me...

MOVING! What do you mean we are moving? There are just moments like this I will never understand. As a child, it is easy not to. Adults do not really need to explain themselves. I wish you would though. I can not believe you are trying to ruin my life with all of your many "Because we said so," comments. That is just not an acceptable answer.

This life and school are all I know! You can not take that away from me. I do not want to leave my friends. If we move away, way out there, I will never see them again. You tell me I will make new friends, that I will see my friends again, but I do not believe you! You are always at work and Dad will not take me. He never wants to do anything for me.

WAIT... WHAT DID YOU JUST SAY? You can not be serious... my sister gets to stay. How, is that fair?!? If she can drive herself to school, why can't she take me to school? Just because she is a senior means nothing! I should be able to have a choice too!

Ugh, I am not getting anywhere with you! As I storm off to my room, I try to think hard of a way to get out of this.

I Miss You!

Love,
Ashley

Dear Mom, It's Me...

Well, you got me to move. I am not very happy about it, but here we are. The house is nice and we have lots of room. Dad is talking about building a pole barn. I am guessing he is going to be working on his guitar stuff, but who knows? I just want to have the pool back. It would be nice if I could swim for part of the summer.

It is a good thing we moved in the summer since we have lots of time to unpack. I only have a month or so before I start school. I can not believe that I will be starting seventh grade at a new school. I am still talking to my old friends, but I will not get to see them as much. We are at least fifteen minutes away from where we were, and that is only by car. If I were to take my bike out, it would be an hour's ride.

The house is set back into the woods. The 10 acres are almost divided. Part of the backyard is nothing but small trees and tall weeds. It is like they never mowed back there. The other part of the acres is the side of the house where the woods are. They are kind of creepy, especially at night. When we went to the open house, they told me that I was being picked up at the end of our driveway early in the morning. I would have to walk down it, in the dark, all by myself. That makes it even more creepy!

There is one thing that is nice about this house. I get to have my own bedroom. Not that I minded sharing, but it is nice to have my own space. That I will enjoy for sure. I wonder if that is why we moved. Did my sister complain and want her own space? I really hope not.

I Miss You!

Love,
Ashley

Dear Mom, It's Me...

I have been in school now for a while. It is not so bad. I have made a couple of new friends. One befriended me on the bus. Did you know that my bus ride is almost an hour each way? It sucks having to get up so early. I have fallen asleep a couple of times already on the bus. They had to turn around and bring me back to school. I felt bad for the bus driver, but she understood.

The funny thing is... I didn't know I had a cousin who was at this school. He mostly hangs out with the "cool kid" crowd. That is not the crowd I belong to. I am not a jock, cheerleader, etc. I would rather hang out with the friends I made. They seem to understand me more.

In the center of one of the hallway, there is a cool seating space for lunch, break, etc. This space is always filled. It is hard to find time to sit between classes too. Next to it, there is a school store. They sell candy, water, pop, pencils, paper, etc.

My teachers kind of treat me like I am an outcast. At this school, you have to be in some type of sport to be noticed.

Being out in the country, you can really smell the farmers doing their thing. The smell gets inside the building all the time. We had to evacuate the other day because the building smelled like gas. There was nothing wrong with it; just smelled from the outside, overpowering the entire building. Tomorrow is another day.

I Miss You!

Love,
Ashley

Chapter 2

Dear Mom, It's Me...

There are times in life when you realize that things happen for a reason. I now understand how that feels. The reason we had to move was because Dad wanted more space and a place out in the country. In this process, I have met so many people and have made a ton of friends. Even though I was not happy about it in the beginning, I am happy now.

The school is bigger than my last one. It feels like all the grade levels are in one location. There are so many people here. I like most of my teachers, but there is one or two that I can not stand. One seems to never leave me alone. It is weird. I do not understand why he continues to pick on me. It is not like that old saying "If someone likes you, they pick on you." I really do not believe that this would be the case.

The hardest part is that he is my math teacher. We both know how much I hate doing math. It would be nice if I had a teacher who was supportive of me and willing to help me. I do not feel that way with him. The nice thing is that my friends helped back me up as well. So, it makes the daily ill treatment tolerable.

So far my grades are good. Yet, at my young age, who

really cares about grades? At this point in my life, I have no idea what I am going to do in the future. It's a factor that I have not even considered as of now.

I Miss You,

Love,
Ashley

Dear Mom, It's Me...

So much for all these friends of mine at school. Today they thought it would be funny to pull me off the stage at school. Three people were involved in it. One held my hand, another held my other hand, and one had a hold of my ankle. When they pulled, I went down on my free foot and bounced. I think they broke it. I do not understand why someone would do this. What are they getting out of hurting me?

I was rolled out of the gym in an office chair. They called you and Dad to come get me. As much as I hate going to the hospital, we went anyway. They told me that I would have to have surgery to correct the broken bone. I remember we went through everything to avoid having surgery. I was on crutches for a while, wore a walking boot, and had my foot wrapped.

The sad thing about all of this is that those so-called friends are not even helping me get around the school. I still want Dad to take me to school so I do not have to get on the bus like this. It was too hard to walk up the steps, and when I was on my crutches, it was even harder getting down the aisle of the bus. Not to mention, it saves me about thirty minutes if Dad takes me. I know it will not last forever, but at least right now I can enjoy being driven around.

I Miss You,

Love,
Ashley

Dear Mom, It's Me...

I met a boy at my school. He is taller than me and very stout. He is super nice and seems to care about me. He is in the same grade as I am. I know Dad would like him compared to my past interests. I do not think he liked my last boyfriend. I am sure it was because he was Mexican. I do not understand how he can be so judgmental. It is not fair.

The nice thing is that this boy has a huge family and I have met most of them. It is nice that he could hang out with his cousins and such as if they were his friends. I am surprised at how quickly we all became friends. I love spending time with all of them. I would have never guessed that I would have so many "brother" type friends in my life.

Some of those guys have friends of their own that we have started to hang out with. I am sure you are aware that this is happening since they are at the house almost every night. I love how they also have adopted me as a little sister. They take really good care of me and always make sure that I am safe. The best part is, I can call them when Dad is being Dad and they are always here in a heartbeat. If anything were to happen to these friendships I would be devastated. I know as people grow older they sometimes drift apart.

I Miss You!!

Love,
Ashley

Dear Mom, It's Me...

The guys and I did something crazy today. We used my friend's station wagon to sled down the driveway. It was so much fun! Since our driveway is so long and we have the turnaround, we were able to enjoy it. We tied the sled to the bumper of the car. At first, we each took a turn to figure out what we were doing. After a while, we started to tie the two sleds to the back so more than one person could go at a time. I remember you and Dad telling us to be careful but to have fun at the same time.

The first time we did it, we were out there until after dark. Thank goodness Dad had that flood light on the shed, otherwise, it would have been dark. The guys are talking about taking our little adventure out on the road. The road is always snow-covered and is hardly ever driven on. I think I will continue to ride in the back, taking pictures/videos of the fun. I do not want to risk hurting myself. We already had one issue with one of the girlfriends. She sprained her wrist rolling off a sled going around the corner. I am not even sure why she is out here. Her boyfriend is my friend and she wants to spend time with him, but this is not something she would normally do. I guess we will see what tomorrow brings.

I Miss You!!

Love,
Ashley

Dear Mom, It's Me...

What an absolute rush! As we had discussed, the guys and I decided to take the sleds on the road. The boys would not let me do any of it (not that I wanted to), but they had fun. At first, we started out going really slow. Then, oh boy did they press down on the gas pedal. It felt like we were doing fifty miles an hour on the road.

I was in the back of the car with the video camera. We had the back hatch open so I could see outside. Starting in the driveway gave us a lot of room to get up to speed as well. However, we had to watch for cars as we were leaving the driveway. Even the neighbors across the street came out to watch.

I worried as we were doing this that the guys would get a rock or something thrown at their eyes. They were out there in just their jeans and coats. They did not have any real protection while doing this. It was interesting to see the spray of the slush on the road go flying from under the tires. All anyone could smell was the exhaust fumes from the car. When it was quiet, you could hear the slush and road noise. It didn't get quite often as we were too busy having fun and yelling at each other. I remember consistently telling them to hold on tight and be very careful. I do not know how they did it, but they did.

Thankfully no one was hurt and we all managed to make it back to the house without an issue. We went inside the house and warmed ourselves. The tingling sensation was leaving our frozen fingers the longer we were inside. Our red noses returned to their normal state but the smiles never left. After our partial warm up we decided to get into the hot tub to officially warm our bodies. It was so much fun having all of us in the hot tub. The hot tub generally seats four people, but in our case, we squished seven people in it.

I remember the last time we were all in the hot tub. You and Dad were not very happy with me after. The boys and I had just gotten back from the Insane Clown Posse concert. We were covered in Fago and decided to jump in for a late-night warm-up. Little did I pay attention at the time that we had created a very pretty crayon box in it. Dad was not happy that he had to clean it out. Oops.

I Miss You!

Love,
Ashley

Dear Mom, It's Me...

You will not believe what the guys and I did today! Eric got sidelined by a school bus at my school. He was picking me up and the bus driver cut him off and smashed the entire side of his red truck. Oh man, was he mad. I have never seen him so upset before. In any case, the insurance company gave him a rental. Giving him the rental was a huge mistake.

It was dark outside and the weather was kind of nice. So, Eric came and picked us all up. It was the last day he was going to have the rental. Now, I have never claimed to be a good child, and this was just way too much fun.

After we had picked everyone up, we went down a few side streets. It was dark outside and we used the car doors as a means of a battering ram. First, we started off with small construction cones and such; then, we went a little bigger to small trees. Later we moved to bigger stuff like garbage cans, mailboxes, etc. You know how we have that small trail next to our house? Yeah, we went down that too, and took out some small trees. It was a riot. He wanted to make an effort to destroy this car before he returned it. I think it was a means to self-satisfaction about what happened to his truck. I do not blame him. I just hope they do not charge him for the damage. I would feel bad if that were the case. Either way, it was still fun. I am sure he will be happy when he gets his truck back. He loves that thing.

I Miss You!!

Love,
Ashley

Dear Mom, It's Me...

The snow is starting to melt. It kind of takes away from the sledding fun. The guys and I are never bored though. We always find something to do. However, the atmosphere has changed with them. It seems like there is a rift somewhere. I think a lot of it is from the assorted girlfriends that come and go. There have been a couple that some of us really do not like to be around. Therefore, it has taken a toll on some of us.

I can not complain too much about it. I also have started seeing a man. I really can refer to him as a man since he is older than me. I am not sure what about him strikes me, but there is something there. It is crazy how you can meet people and never really know whether you and that person will be together in the long run or not. He is older than me and still lives at his mom's house. He is cute to a point but I have never really judged a book by its cover. I am not much better. I am not really sure what is going to happen, but for now, I will enjoy my time with him.

I am really surprised that you are allowing me to date someone so much older than me. I often wondered if you trusted me that much or were trying to teach me a lesson. However, at this point, I am not sure what that lesson would be.

I Miss You!

Love,
Ashley

Dear Mom, It's Me...

You know how I have been spending all this time with my boyfriend? Well, I really do like him. I almost wonder if I love him. We spent so much time together and his mom is ok with me hanging out over there. We watch movies together, go for walks, go out to eat, and do all sorts of couple-like things. His friend comes over every once in a while and we all hang out as a group too. It is a lot of fun.

The other night we did something. I often wonder if it was the right choice. Mom, I have lost my virginity to him. It was an interesting experience. It was not as painful as all my friends told me it would be. I rather enjoyed it. Yet, at this point, I have nothing to compare it to, but was still not bad.

The state of his mom's house is not all that great. He does not have a room to himself so his bed is on the floor in the laundry area. I am not sure if it was supposed to be a room or not, but still. He does not even have a bed - it is more of a mattress on the floor. I suppose that some people live very different lives than others.

The one thing that I am afraid of with this adventure is that I am not on any form of birth control. I highly doubt that I could get pregnant on my first experience, can I? Is that even possible? Goodness, I really hope not. I wish I felt more comfortable talking to you about this. In some ways, I am worried that you will be disappointed in me for the choices that I have made. In any case...

I Miss You!!

Love,
Ashley

Dear Mom, It's Me...

Today was the day that changed my entire life. My boyfriend and his mom took me to the health department. I needed to get verification on something. As it turns out, your fifteen-year-old daughter is pregnant. I guess I quickly discovered what it is that I am going to do with the rest of my life. I would have never imagined that this was what I would be doing. Now the big question prevails. How do I tell you and Dad? I hope you will still love me.

I Miss You!

Love,
Ashley

Chapter 3

Dear Mom, It's Me...

I do not think that I have ever been this scared in my life. I am pregnant and now feel like I do not have anyone to help me. I am afraid of talking to you about it because I know Dad will find out. I know how dad is and I am afraid he will go crazy. I do not want him to hurt me again.

I am trying to go to school. Yet, it is hard to focus. School is the same old thing every day. I know I was not trying very hard and I have missed a lot. Well, okay I have skipped school a lot, but isn't that what kids do these days?

I have told my closest friends about what is going on. They have been very supportive of me. I am thankful for that. They also understand my fears by telling you. I am thankful that I have my friends.

I have not really had any symptoms as of yet, well, short of missing my period. Other than that, I feel fine. As you know, I have been hiding out at my boyfriend's house. I am not sure what else to do. His mom has been good to me. She is constantly talking about her soon-to-be grandchild. It is nice, but at the same time, I wish I had the same comments from you. I can only hope that you will be just as happy when you do find out. Getting tired right now, I think I am going to call it a night. I love you!!

I Miss You!!

Love,
Ashley

Dear Mom, It's Me...

I was walking the hall today to another class when I happened to glance through the office windows and saw you standing there. I questioned why you were not at work. As I walked into the office, I saw that look on your face. Shit, have you found out?

You proceeded to give me the third degree on why I was missing school. I know that my boyfriend's mom forgot to call me in one day. I am guessing you had a conversation with the school to discuss my absences. Many of these days I am just at his house. I really did not want to go to school. It is not so much because I am pregnant, it is mostly because I do not like going to school.

In any case, I stood there lying to your face. Telling you that I was sick, vomiting up blood, and had a fever. I can see by the look on your face that you were not buying it. I had to think of something quick.

At this point, I can only promise you that I will come home after school on the bus. Ugh, I already had plans but I guess I have to change them now.

As I try to go on with my day, I know that something is cooking at home. I knew that one day I would have to face it, but was hoping for more time.

I Miss You!!!

Love,
Ashley

Dear Mom, It's Me...

I wonder if your questioning came from the other day when we were at dinner at Aunt K's house. It was Christmas dinner and we were sitting around the table. I had to pee and wanted to get up. I was contemplating in my head whether I should get up normally or act like a pregnant woman. I chose the wrong route. Wow, did everyone give me a look. I thought "Oh shit, I am dead." As I got up and dealt with all the looks, I pretended that I had a backache but we all know that was not the case.

I remember that as I came back from the bathroom and sat down you still had that look on your face. I have a feeling you already knew, but I will have to deal with that when the time comes. At this point, even though I just found out I am pregnant, I am more than likely a couple of months along. I am due in August. Summer pregnancy is going to be interesting; by then I will be as fat as a bull.

I really hope that you have not been going through my room/closet. That is where I have everything hidden. I do not know if I am as good as you at hiding things but we will see. As long as you have not been snooping, I should be okay.

I Miss You!!

Love,
Ashley

Dear Mom, It's Me...

The bomb has dropped. Dad paced back and forth outside of my room. He screamed something at the top of his lungs. I could not really make it out. I sat on my bed crying because you found the pamphlets and such that I had hidden in my closet. When you came into my room I knew something was up. You had them all in your hand and proceeded to ask me over and over again if I was pregnant. Damn.

Dad was going over and over again about how "That boy will work for me the rest of his life." Like that would happen. He already has a job so why would he need to go work for him? You have managed to keep him out of my room as of right now. I know that you understand that I am more afraid of him than I am of telling you the truth.

As you proceeded to drill me for an honest answer, I gave in. Through all of my tears, I finally came clean and said, "Yes Mom, it is true. I am pregnant." What else was there to say? At this point, I am already six months along and I have been good at hiding it. I know that I am not the skinniest person in the world but my fat has helped me out big time.

Honestly, at this time I feel so much better. I have been able to tell you the truth and that everything will be better. I am sure Dad is going to fester on this as long as he can but I know you are not mad at me. Right now, that is all that matters. I can only wonder what is to come now. I plan to stay at school as long as I can.

I Miss You!!

Love,
Ashley

Dear Mom, It's Me...

Today, you told me that we were going out for lunch. I am excited about this because I know that we will talk about everything and it will be okay. We went to Burger King to eat. I have been craving Burger King all the time. Right now, this is really the only symptom that I have. Not bad for being six months pregnant and only eating constantly. After we ate, you dragged me to a doctor's office. I guess I should have known that this was going to happen. I can not be mad. I know you are just looking out for my best interests.

As we are completing the paperwork, my stomach starts to act up. I had to run to the bathroom a couple of times. I should have known better than to eat what I had. It went right through me. I also think that it could be my nerves as well. I had no idea what was going to happen.

The nurse came out and gathered me to bring me back to the room. She asked me a few questions about what was going on and how long ago since I was told I was pregnant. The look on your face told me everything that I knew already. I think you and Dad wanted me to come here to "get rid of" the baby but you realized that it is too late. I hope that is not the case but sometimes with you and Dad I never know. I am sure at this point you are embarrassed that your now sixteen-year-old daughter is pregnant. I am really sorry, but honestly, this could be a good thing.

I Miss You!!

Love,
Ashley

Dear Mom, It's Me...

Well, the doctor's visit went well. They told me that the baby looked and sounded good. They told me that I was a bit dehydrated and should drink lots of water for the next couple of days. That is going to be hard because you know that I am a very serious pop drinker. The doctor also told me that it would be healthier for me and the baby if I quit smoking. This will be a challenge, but I am sure I can do it.

After we returned home, I was still frustrated with the whole situation. Dad still has an attitude with me and just keeps mumbling under his breath. I am sure it is going to take him a while to accept the situation. Trust me, I am still trying to get used to the situation too.

School is about to let out soon. I am not quite showing yet, so it is still easier to hide it. Only my closest friends know what is happening, and they often wonder if I will come back to school next year. I kind of wonder the same thing. Having a baby over the summer makes me question what is going to happen after the fact.

I have not really been hanging out with the guys anymore. I guess that happens when people find someone that they care about romantically. They abandoned me a long time ago.

This does make me very sad because we were all really close, but at this point, there is nothing I can do about it. As time goes on, people change, situations change, and life changes.

I Miss You!!

Love,
Ashley

Dear Mom, It's Me...

I just got home from the doctor's office. They told me that this little one is being very stubborn. At this point, I am a week overdue. They told me that if I do not go into labor naturally then they will have to induce me. I just sat there with my eyes wide open, trying to figure out what it was they just told me. I am 16 years old, how am I supposed to know what inducing means? They are giving me the rest of the week, then they are going to schedule it.

My sister and you have been getting things ready for the baby. It makes me feel good to know that you are no longer angry with me. We were talking about repainting my room but I do not think we will have enough time.

Do you remember when I sponged my room that day? I wanted my room to look like the sky. So, I took a sponge and started painting my room. I am sure that it was just a fluke that I wanted it like that but it is cute all the same.

We put the crib in my room along with all the baby stuff. In a way; I am kind of excited to have the baby here. I know most pregnant women say that, especially after a summer pregnancy. It really is not easy. I know that there have been many times that I have sweated through my clothes just sitting in a restaurant and at home. We do not have air conditioning but I have been bathing in the pool a lot to cool down. I guess we just need to wait to see what the rest of the week brings.

I Miss You!!!

Love,
Ashley

Dear Mom, It's Me...

Today is the day. They have scheduled me to get induced. Apparently, it is administered in the form of a pill that they put on my cervix to start the labor process. I guess it agitates the cervix to thin out enough to go into labor. I am not looking forward to this at all. You and my boyfriend climbed into the car with me. We checked into the hospital and were brought to the room. They had me change into a gown and the doctor came in to put the pill in. They said it should only be a matter of time before things start to happen.

After an hour or so of being there, you decided to go home for whatever reason. It got dark out, so I knew that it was getting late. They had asked me to get up and started walking around. There are only so many interesting things that I could look at on this one floor. I wish I could walk more in other places but they tell me to stay on this floor, just in case.

I have gone to the bathroom many times, but this time it feels different. Ohh, man. It feels like I have to have a bowel movement, but can not. Oh the cramps are kicking in, I think that it is getting closer to time. I am screaming in the bathroom at the nurse to get me every drug they have. They already know what is going on. They asked me if I wanted an epidural. I told them I did.

After less than an hour, the anesthesiologist came in with his tray of goodies. The nurse sat me up on the bed and they told me to lean down towards my knees. This was the first time I had ever had a needle in my back. It was not the most comfortable thing to experience. Once the doctor found the right location and got the needle inserted the pain relief began and I could not be more grateful.

The doctor told us that it should not be too much longer before the real labor began. I lay in bed very comfortably and watched TV. I felt some pressure down there, but nothing too unbearable. The doctor came in and out to check to see how dilated I was. He eventually informed the nurse that he needed to start preparing for birth. They brought in a plastic, portable crib with a blanket, etc. in it. They also brought in a tray for tools and other supplies.

After about a half hour, the doctor and nurses came back in again and told me it was time. I do not remember much of it except that you were not there and came in a while after. I remember the baby being born and was told that I have a healthy, eight-pound, seven-ounce baby. He is really cute.

I was in the hospital through most of the following day. They told me they wanted to keep an eye on me to ensure that the baby was eating well and I was healing. I'm excited to go home and take a shower in my own bathroom.

As you can imagine, I am tired, so I am going to sleep now before they bring the baby back in.

I Miss You!!

Love,
Ashley

Dear Mom, It's Me...

It has been a few weeks since the baby was born. He is so small, I can not believe it. You and my sister planned a baby shower. You asked me to get together all the names of people that I would like to invite. Naturally, that consists of my family and a couple of friends that I still have. It is hard to maintain friends when you have an infant child, but those who really care about me are still coming over. It is the end of August and I decided not to go back to school next year. So, we can have a shower whenever it works.

A couple of weeks later we had a shower. The majority of the women here are family, but a few of my friends showed up. I have been passing around the baby like crazy. In some ways, it is nice to have my arms relaxed, but in another way, I want my baby back.

It was a really nice shower. I got a bunch of clothes for the baby and a few larger objects that were needed. It does help not working. I know that you have been spending money on the little one like crazy. I appreciate that. I am not sure I ever really said that to you. I wish I could now.

I Miss You!!

Love,
Ashley

Loss & Lost
2003 – 2004

Chapter 4

Dear Mom, It's Me...

My sister came to pick me up today. She said that Dad needed us. I am not sure what is going on. When she got here, she was sullen. She didn't say much on the way to our destination. The ride felt like it took forever. We were on the highway and it was cold outside. The fall day was so pretty. The sun was getting ready to set and the twilight sky glowed a mix of purple, orange, and yellow. The clouds on the horizon looked like big, puffy pillows floating in the sky.

We arrived at a tall building. I couldn't really determine the name of it until we were right on top of it. We pulled into a dark parking garage. I thought the little Honda was going to be squished. The ceiling was creeping up to the top of the car. We found a parking spot and began walking toward the building. The building got larger the closer we walked to it. That's when I figured out that this was a hospital. I knew you were not feeling good so it does not surprise me that we were there.

We got up to the room you were staying in. You are in the bed and Dad is sitting next to you. His eyes were red and swollen. I could tell he had been crying, but why? It wasn't long before I found out what was going on. You told us you have had some testing done and the news was not good. The dreaded feeling was bursting in my guts. I know what that means. We joined you on your bed. I sat on the edge and my sister was closer to you and Dad.

Cancer, you have cancer. Not just in one spot. You told me that you have liver and pancreatic cancer. What? Why?? Shock and awe take over my body. I can't move. I am frozen on the end of this lumpy hospital bed. All I can do is stare at you, Dad, and my sister. She started to cry and cuddled up closer to you. Dad began to cry again and I knew that this was serious. He is always angry and his face always looks pissed off. This was really a different side of him. Dad told us you are going to fight this and that everything will be ok. We sat for a while with you as you further explained what was going to happen and what the doctors had told you so far. I was still in shock.

I often wonder if you knew that there were secrets to this situation that you were not telling us. That there was more that we should have known. It is easy to say that everything will be ok and not have to disclose anything further. I know you are trying to protect us from the hurt and the pain but really it is not fair.

I Miss You!!

Love,
Ashley

Dear Mom, It's Me...

I wonder if my sister should have been driving home tonight. Her eyes are red and her face is puffy from crying. She maintains the speed limit as we slink down the highway. It is dark out and the moon is in the sky. I remember years ago when you dressed up as the moon man for Halloween. The big blue moon in the sky reminds me of this time. A small smile crosses my face at this thought and I maintain it all the way home.

My tears have yet to pour out as we arrive back home. The boys are there waiting for me to come in through the door. The smiles on their faces seem to lighten up the glooming cloud hanging over me. I love how they are always so excited when I get home.

As I start to get the kids ready for bed, I am eager for you to come home. I know that it will only be a couple of days and I hope that you will be here forever. That this is just a dream and nothing that happened tonight will be real in the morning. I guess we will see. Good night!

I Miss You!!

Love,
Ashley

Dear Mom, It's Me...

I am so glad you are home. It's been weird with you not here. It seems like you practically brought the hospital home with you. There are so many different things on the counter now. I am sure this is all to keep you healthy, so I will deal with it.

It is amazing how despite all this medication and having this disease going on inside of you are still willing to go back to your daily routine. I don't think it is a good idea to be working, but I know that is one thing that can't be taken away from you. But I know it will not last long.

I wish there was a way to tell the boys, but I know they will not understand. They are too young to even know what Cancer is, let alone the body parts that it has taken over. I guess one day when they are older, I will tell them what happened to you. The worst part is my youngest is so little that he won't even get a chance to know his grandma. He is so little and already loves you very much. You've done a great job helping me with them and it is hard to think they won't have you for longer.

As you rest easy in your chair, I am leaning on the wall, watching you sleep. News like this changes my perspective on life and my relationship with you. I know that I wasn't always the best daughter, let alone the best behaved, but I am thankful that I have always had you.

I Miss You!!

Love,
Ashley

Dear Mom, It's Me....

Today was your first doctor's appointment following your visit to the hospital. Only today, it wasn't with your regular physician, it was with the cancer doctor. I am sure you were as nervous to hear what they had to say as I was. The office is kind of a small space; it's warm but does not feel as inviting as most doctors' offices. The chairs are uncomfortable and it's hot inside. I guess with it being so cold out, that makes sense.

In the waiting room, there are pamphlets everywhere talking about options, different types of cancer, and ways to improve your living with cancer. The depth of information is overwhelming. I am not sure if this is making me more uncomfortable, more nervous, or unsure of what is going to happen.

They called you back, but I was forced to stay put. Dad went with you as you walked down the hall into the room. I felt like I'd already been here all day, but now it felt like the time was going even slower. After what felt like hours, you walked out of the room and I was not sure what to think at that point. I saw a bunch of paperwork in your hands and knew that you would be reading most of the night. Well, if you could stay awake.

I hope that this is nothing and we can go on as a semi-happy family. I want my boys to know their grandmother, and life wouldn't seem right without you.

I Miss You!!

Love,
Ashley

Dear Mom, It's Me...

Today was a hard day. My mind could not settle down. My head was spinning out of control. It is like being in a dream world, where you don't know the difference between reality and fantasy. I know that this is just my mind trying to cope with the situation. Yet, I still don't want it to be true.

I have been at work all day and am very concerned for you. When I woke up to get ready you were home. I was surprised, you had been going to work regularly at this point. Yet, this morning you were very sick and tired. It was hard to see and watch. When you don't know what to do for someone you love who is in pain, it breaks your heart. Since Dad doesn't really work, I am glad he is home taking care of you.

Why does cancer have to be so hard on the body? I wonder if the idea of chemo is a good idea. Isn't it another type of poison that is going into your body? I mean, it is trying to kill the cancer, why wouldn't it affect you? In a way, it is because you are more sick than you seemed before the treatment. I can only hope that this gets better for you. I don't like seeing you this way. You were always so spunky and full of life and you worked your butt off.

There has always been so much that I needed to say to you but never dared to do so. I know that I was not always the best child and was in trouble often. I appreciate everything you have done to ensure that I was a happy child. I have never had a want for anything in my life. Somedays I think that with you being sick. you worked too hard for my sister and me. I hope that this is not the reason why this is happening to you. That would make me feel horrible.

I am still not sure how to feel about this situation. Is it going to get worse before it gets better? I still wonder if there is more to this that you are not telling us. I know you are trying not to hurt us, but I think it would hurt us more if you didn't tell us the entire story. I guess being ignorant is better than being totally hurt by the truth. It's like they say... ignorance is bliss.

I Miss You!!

Love,
Ashley

Dear Mom, It's Me...

The days are getting harder and harder. I sit back and watch you go through the pain. Even though I do not live at home, my sister often updates me on what is happening. I try to come home and see you, but seeing you sick like this just does not sit well with me. I don't know what it is. Just being at home with you makes me feel like this is more real to me. I am also scared that I am going to lose you, and I don't want that. I try to come as often as I can, but I don't feel like it is good for the boys to see you like this.

Your stomach is starting to look like you have swallowed a bowling ball. I am finding out as this is going on that you are having a hard time going number two. I wanted to help. So, today I went to Sam's Club and found this very pretty crystal vase. I got the crazy idea of filling this with your favorite candy (M&M's). I decided to use green pipe cleaners to make flowers. I added a couple of different colors to the top of the pipe cleaners for petals. It almost looked like an array of flowers in a dirt-filled vase. I know how much you love M&M's, and generally chocolate makes anyone go to the bathroom.

When I brought it into the house, you smiled. You already knew what I was thinking. I am so glad you liked it. I laughed when I saw the next day that you had put it in your room. I hope this helps; I really do. I am glad I could make you smile for a minute and bring you some joy. Feel better Mom.

I Miss You!!

Love,
Ashley

Dear Mom, It's Me...

I was surprised when I got home today. You had gone to the doctor's to have them drain the ever-growing fluid in your stomach. They told you that this would happen again and you will likely have to go back to have it done again. I was hoping that you would not have to go through the draining process again. That was bizarre. You seem like you are feeling a little better. Your numbers are sort of improving, but it is still kind of early to tell.

Since your long, blonde, curly hair started to fall when you showered, you decided to call your sister today to have her come over and cut your hair. I am surprised that you are willing to cut it so short. I couldn't believe how much hair she cut off. You still had a lot left to keep. It's sad, really, because I have never seen you with short hair like this. She cut the back to around an inch and the top is about five inches. It looks nice though. Still, it going to take some getting used to.

We decided to do a 'before and after' picture. You had the biggest smile on your face. I am so glad that you were at least happy about this. I would have been in tears and hiding under the covers. Changes as big as this would not have gone well for me. Your sister seems happy with it too, which is good because I don't want to hear the sisterly brutal truth kind of love later. I am so proud of you Mom. I know you can do this.

I Miss You!!

Love,
Ashley

2004

Chapter 5

Dear Mom, It's Me...

Even after all you are going through, I am surprised that you still want to go to Florida. I know my sister and I both have misgivings about it. You promised us that everything would be fine and you would still be getting your chemo treatments while you were there. I do not know if being around so many people is such a good idea for you. What happens if you get sick, hurt, or something worse?

You and Dad left anyway. I know you have been busy down there because you are sending packages home. I am guessing since you two flew down, it is easier to send home stuff, versus having it on the plane.

Dad was telling us that you tried to see the Orange County Chopper people, and they were not very nice to you. I guess, that is what happens when you let fame go to your head. I can not understand why, even with all of your friends telling them you are sick with cancer, they continued. Either way, I am glad you are having fun. That is what is important right now - being happy and having a good time.

I Miss You!

Love,
Ashley

Dear Mom, It's Me...

At this point, it seems like going to Florida was a good idea. However, you have gone downhill since then. Your skin is starting to sink into your body. You are so thin. The only thing that still shows part of you is your stomach. It has gotten big again. If I ever get in this sort of a position, I do not want to go through the same thing you are. I know you are doing everything you can to get better and it is not going to be easy. However, I feel like this is a battle you will not win. That scares me.

Dad told me that it would not be long before hospice had to come in. In a few weeks, you will be fifty years old. I have a feeling that there is going to be a surprise birthday party for you. I worry that you will not be able to go. I worry that you will be too sick to go, and I am sure that Dad feels the same way. We would not want to put you in an uncomfortable position. We want you to be able to enjoy what you are doing and be able to celebrate with everyone. I think it is going to be at Fricano's. I wonder who will be there. I guess we will see what happens.

I Miss You!

Love,
Ashley

Dear Mom, It's Me...

The birthday party was good. You were smiling and having a good time. It was nice to see all of your friends there. We had plenty to eat thanks to the guys you used to work with. That pizza always upsets my stomach, but in the end, it was worth it. I worry that this will be the last time you can get up and be outside of the house. When we got home, you were very tired. I know that it took a lot out of you.

The six months that they gave you are starting to come to an end. I can see it in your face, eyes, skin, etc. Your body is changing and it is not for the better. I can see it in Dad's face that he is worried about you. I totally understand. We can see it in the changes that are taking place. I have a feeling it will not be long before we see hospice in the house.

I Miss You!

Love,
Ashley

Dear Mom, It's Me...

Hospice came in and put up a bed in the living room for you. You have been pretty immobile lately. I am not sure what is worse, the fact that you are getting sicker or having to watch you lay in this living room/hospital bed all by yourself. I have my doubts that Dad will be out there with you.

Dad had them put the bed in the same spot as where your chair was. I know you were always comfortable there and it made it easy to watch TV and look out the window. I miss those windows. It was always scary when we watched *Jurassic Park*. We could always see the dinosaurs' reflection in the glass. I remember getting so freaked out one time that there might be an actual dinosaur outside. I was young though. I know better now.

As you lay in that bed, I often wonder what it is you see. You always seem to be looking up at something. Dad thinks that you are looking at the angels. He tells us that sometimes you are talking in your sleep. He often wonders if that is who you are talking to. I can imagine when you are so close to death, your senses are heightened.

I Miss You!

Love,
Ashley

Dear Mom, It's Me...

At this point, I have moved out with my youngest son's Dad again. This will be the last time by the time everything is over. I should have never moved out in the first place. I should have stayed home to help Dad and be with you. I think the idea of you dying has gotten to me and I am scared.

In any case, after getting the boys to bed, I started to get ready for bed myself. Sadly enough, Dad called and told me that you had stopped breathing. I really did not know what to say. I said I was sorry to him and told him that I would be over shortly. The apartment complex is not that far from you.

I told my boyfriend what was going on and asked him to watch the boys. I told him I would be back later, not sure what time later, but later. He understood and I left. It did not take me too long to get there. Everyone that was coming was already there. I often wonder how they beat me. Dad was sitting by your bedside, holding your hand, while everyone else was kind of standing around you. Again, this is where I say... it is always hard to really be able to talk to you alone. There always seems to be someone else too.

So, I am doing my best to be there and keep my shit together. It is not easy. I do not know whether to be mad, sad, or angry. I am just walking in and trying to gain my perspective on the situation. All everyone around me is doing is crying. Which, I understand, but at the same time, I am waiting for you to wake up and say it was all a joke. I have my doubts that this will happen. One can only hope.

A little while after I got there, hospice came in. They confirmed the time of death and called the morgue. They needed to come to pick you up and bring you to their location. By late in the morning, everyone left and I went home to see my boys and get some sleep. It was a long night.

I Miss You!

Love,
Ashley

Dear Mom, It's Me...

Well, it is the day after you passed. Yet, the world has seemed to stop. I do not know what to do with myself. I am supposed to go to work, but I do not want to. How is that going to affect me? Will I be able to focus on what I need to do? Probably not. The best part about this job is that I work alone on the weekends, so I should be able to just sit alone with my thoughts.

I am sure in a few days Dad is going to be making arrangements for your service. You wanted to be cremated, and that is what is planned. I am sure Dad is going to want to do a service. There were so many people in your life who loved you and wanted to be a part of your life. That is one thing - we are going to have to warn the funeral home about. That your funeral is going to be packed. We will have to see what they come up with. I am sure Dad will be letting us know what is happening and when soon enough. For now, all I can do is try to continue with my life and hope for the best.

I Miss You!

Love,
Ashley

Dear Mom, It's Me...

Well, it is like I thought. Dad said to meet him at the funeral home. Not so easy with two little ones, but they went with me anyway. They were actually well-behaved. I am so thankful that they were. I am sure you had a great deal to do with this as well. You were always wonderful with my kids. I worry that they are missing out on your presence now.

Off to the funeral home we went. Dad wanted to go over the details with us while he was there. It will be a couple of days before the service. This will give all your friends and our family time to get here. There are a lot of people who live further away, which is going to make it harder to gather quickly. I am pretty sure that the time is appreciated.

I often wonder what Dad does now when he gets home. It did not take him long to clean out the house and have his girlfriend over, so who knows? If she shows up to the funeral, there is going to be an outright brawl on our hands. That is for sure.

I Miss You!

Love,
Ashley

Dear Mom, It's Me...

Today was the funeral. I was sitting right up front with Dad and my sister. I had a friend watching the boys. I did not feel comfortable bringing them to the funeral. I did not want them to have PTSD. This is hard enough for me. It is not something that they need to experience yet. I only hope that as they get older it will be easier for them to understand.

I sat there crying and crying as I listened to the priest talk. When your friends stood up to say something, that is when I really lost it. Hearing about times you spent happy with your friends, the silly things you did, and everything that you meant to them. I know that you have touched many people in your lifetime, but I had no idea that there was such a connection between you and some of these people.

I was right though. This place is packed with everyone you knew. I am so happy to see some of my friends here who knew who you were, and I am thankful they are there for me as well.

They had to open the other room so everyone would fit into the service. They even set up a TV in the room so everyone was able to watch the service if they were not able to see all the way to the front. I am sure they appreciated it. I could not even see who was in the other room. My eyes were so swollen and full of tears. I am not sure I could even see straight. It was hard to look at everyone while they were talking. I just kept crying.

Before I knew it, everyone was standing up and the parade of people and hugs began. It is a good thing that I already had a headache because you know how the smells would affect me. I get through it, say goodbye to the family, and make my way home. Once we arrived I kissed my kids, said goodbye to my friend, and hit the bed. I lay there for several days.

I Miss You!

Love,
Ashley

Chapter 6

Dear Mom, It's Me...

I spent several days in bed. I could not get myself to get up. I took a couple of days off from work to make sure I was available. Although, with everything going on, I am not so sure I was needed anyway. I personally think Dad is trying to keep me away from the house. I know exactly why. He knows that I will have something to say about what he is doing. I am not afraid of him any longer and do not really care. The thing is, he has been acting weird and I do not know or understand why.

The funeral home called and told us that your ashes are in. Yet, Dad will not go pick them up. What does he think is going to happen? That you will just get up and walk home? I do not understand why he is acting this way. In any case, he talked to your sister and she went to go get you. Sadly, it had to be either her or him, otherwise, my sister and/or I would have gone. The odd thing is that your ashes did not come home. Dad had your sister hold onto them.

I Miss You!

Love,
Ashley

Dear Mom, It's Me...

The house is so strange without you in it. I have moved back home again. My last relationship ended badly, and I had Dad come get me. I was scared and knew that I needed to get out before something bad happened. We moved all my stuff in a big hurry. Some of it went downstairs (since my sister is not there any longer) and some stuff is in the barn.

I am not happy being home again but I had nowhere else to go. While I do appreciate the fact that Dad came and got me and moved me back home, I know he does not want me here. I am glad the boys will have more space to move around and go outside to do things. It makes it a lot nicer for them to play. I still have Bear with me. I am not going to let her go. For a dog, she is amazing with the boys and pretty much lets them do whatever they want. This is important in a breed. I hope that she lives forever.

I Miss You!

Love,
Ashley

Dear Mom, It's Me...

The odd thing about living here again is that I can feel your presence in the house. The boys and I are in the living room now. For the most part, this is where they play. It is still very weird. I can hardly look towards the door and not picture you there in that bed. It is haunting.

I woke up to the neighbor across the street this morning banging on the door. I was really surprised to see her there. She had Bear on a rope. I asked, "What is going on?" She told me that Bear was in her barn, chasing her chickens. I took my dog and apologized and said I hoped that she did not do any damage. She is such a nice lady. I so appreciated her kindness. I have a feeling that Dad let her out this morning on purpose. He has made it apparent that he does not want her here. I know he was really bothered when Sheba died, but come on. He knows how much this dog means to me. I do not know why he would hurt me and the boys like that. I am just glad she is home.

I Miss You!

Love,
Ashley

Dear Mom, It's Me...

Working on just the weekends is starting to get to me. The boys are in so many different sports and most of the games are on Saturdays. It is hard to get a day off to go see them, especially when I work alone in the office. This company has gone through so many site managers I am losing count. One would think that this says something about the people they hire to run this place.

The thing is, I do like it here. I have met so many special people and most of the residents love me. It is almost like having an extended family that I see on the weekends. During the week, I started working at the outlet mall office. I really like it there too. The manager lets me do my homework while I am at work, and I am pretty free to do whatever is needed. The only thing he requests is that I answer the phone and do my other duties. I think that is fair enough.

I Miss You!

Love,
Ashley

Dear Mom, It's Me...

The weather is starting to change. The leaves on all the trees are changing color. I almost forget every time how beautiful it is out here. Driving to the house and leaving, no matter which way you go, you can see the bright oranges, reds, and greens on the trees. Every time I leave I just can't help but look around. It is really amazing. Even looking out the back yard I can see right over the rubbish and the trees are just as beautiful. I am really going to miss it here. I have a feeling that Dad will sell the house at some point. He does not like to take care of all of it by himself. I do some of the work, but between working and the boys, I do not have a lot of extra time.

It will be nice to use the pool one more time before we possibly move. I think out of everything here that is the one thing I adore having the most. The pool is right in the backyard and I do not have to go anywhere to swim. The only thing I can hope for is that Grandma never closes her pool.

I Miss You!

Love,
Ashley

Dear Mom, It's Me...

The days seem to just sit still. Time does not move forward. The clock ticks by while I pretend that everything is perfect. However, nothing is perfect. You are no longer here.

I do not understand how people move on as they do. I feel like I will be living in this darkness forever. This was truly something I never would have imagined would happen. I understand that in time every child is supposed to bury their parents. I would not have imagined that I would be doing so with you at only fifty years old.

My birthday will never mean anything to me anymore. This post-traumatic stress syndrome will last forever. It haunts me daily. The days feel dark and gloomy. My usual routine has kept me going. I have just been working as much as I can and spending time with the boys. It is hard to believe that my baby is almost two years old. I was thankful that you were able to attend his one-year birthday party. I just wish they had more time with you.

I Miss You!

Love,
Ashley

Dear Mom, It's Me...

Today your friends took me out for my birthday dinner. It was so nice of them to do that. I know that it is hard on them too. I just turned twenty-one years old. They wanted to take me out to celebrate. My sister was there too. It was good to spend time with everyone. However, the empty space that still looms is horrible.

They gave me the choice of where I wanted to go. Naturally, I chose Applebee's since they have a variety of drinks to choose from. They also have a variety of food that I really enjoy. My sister picked me up and brought me there. I am guessing she thought that I was going to drink heavily, but that was not the case. I have already drank my fair share of liquor until this point. I remember so many nights when I had to call you to come get my son because I drank a little too much beforehand and needed to sleep. I was so grateful when you were able to do that for me. I think at that point I had learned all I needed to about drinking. I am glad that I no longer do such things to myself.

I Miss You!

Love,
Ashley

Dear Mom, It's Me...

I just wanted to check it. I really do not know what to write about today. Life has become very stagnant. It seems like the only thing I do is work, take care of the boys, and go to school. I try to do what I can for their sports, but as I said before, it is hard to work like I am. I do try. I hope that one day they understand that. I also hope that they never have to suffer as I have been. I guess all I can do is hope for the best for them. That is the only thing any mom can do.

I Miss You!

Love,
Ashley

Chapter 7

Dear Mom, It's Me...

Dad informed me today that he was selling the house. I can understand why it bothers him to live here. I swear, there have been many times I was walking through the house and a dark shadow appeared. I could have sworn it was you. The hallway was dark and I could not see. I ran into something and freaked out then ran back to my bedroom. I quickly turned on the light and was sad to see it was in my head.

He told me and my sister that we needed to start cleaning out the house. I am sure your sisters and mom will be here to help with that. I just hope that he does not go through everything and throw things away. There are so many things here that could be worth money and/or are just awesome keepsakes. Not to mention I know how much you liked to hide money all over the place.

It is really hard living here with him without you. There are several memories in this house that I will soon forget.

I Miss You!

Love,
Ashley

Dear Mom, It's Me...

Today, I came home and the house was a mess. Dad has already started to go through your stuff. It's been about a week since we lost you.

There is stuff everywhere. It is like he was bored and just decided to go through everything. He said your sister will be here soon and your mother too. Great.

About 20 minutes later, I found myself sitting on the steps towards the downstairs. My sister was down there with me. Dad was upstairs there with his new girlfriend, and I did not want to be a part of that. I have never seen her before. She seems awfully comfortable in the house. It almost seems like she has been here before.

As I made my way up the stairs, I noticed the crystal vase that I got you. It was sitting on the counter. As I go to grab it, a voice behind me says, "That is mine." I turned around and there she was. She was trying to tell me that she was taking it. I went to snap back at her, but Dad was right there with that horrible look on his face. The same look I have seen many times. Especially those times that I would rather forget. So, I turned on my heels and walked back downstairs to speak to my sister.

Your mom and sisters were downstairs with me. I started crying and felt hurt. I could not believe he was doing this. I got you that vase because you were having a hard time. I wanted to keep it. It meant more to me than anything at this point. It was more than just a vase to me.

I did not know how this man was able to hurt me twice in one day without laying a finger on me this time.

I Miss You!!

Love,
Ashley

Dear Mom, It's Me...

I am alone living with Dad now. Today, my sister moved out and bought her first house. I am happy for her, but at the same time, that leaves me home with him. He doesn't scare me anymore, but he still hurts me both mentally and emotionally.

I am not sure if she moved out, because she met someone or if it is because we are moving. The house that Dad is looking to buy is old, grungy, and looks like a barn. It has two floors. The floor upstairs is one huge loft with a small bedroom, which looks more like a walk-in closet. There is a bedroom downstairs, which Dad will sleep in.

The house has red carpeting with wood-looking walls. It is kind of ugly. The kitchen is a mess. Dad seems to think we can live here while he works on it. What a nightmare. He is going to build a house next to it and then do something with this one.

I do not want to move. I really like it out here. Especially with the pool and hot tub. With my sister gone, it is going to be harder.

I Miss you!

Love,
Ashley

Dear Mom, It's Me...

Today, the moving truck is here. We are doing most of it ourselves but there are a few others here as well. I still do not want to move. Dad says if I want to live at home, then I have no choice but to move with him. So, the boys and I started to move our stuff. It is a lot of work getting everything up the stairs at the new house. The steps are red and wooden so they are slippery.

At the top of the stairs, it turns into a trapezoid tread. These stairs are bigger and wider than the others. The problem is they curve a bit. Most of my furniture will not fit going up. I had to replace the box spring on my bed with two single ones. Bear has a hard time on the slippery steps too. She is getting older and it is harder to walk for her to walk. Dad was being a jerk about her coming with me, but I was not going to give up my dog for him. I love her and have had her for several years. Regardless, there is more crap I have to put up with.

He has made me his maid now too. I have to clean the house because he will not. He expects me to clean so that I do not pay rent. He also has his girlfriends coming and going as we are moving. I do not understand why he would do this. First, I lose you. Then, my sister moved. Now, I have to deal with all this. I do not mind the move but I worry about my boys and how this is going to impact them. I do not want them to think that consistently moving is going to be a part of their lives. I guess we will see how this goes. I know I can not afford to live on my own.

I Miss You!!

Love,
Ashley

Dear Mom, It's Me...

We have all moved in. Dad is hell-bent on building a house next to this one. I do not understand why. What is the point? He claims he is going to do this all by himself, but I have my doubts.

He told me that if I ever moved out or moved in with my boyfriend, that all of "this" would no longer be mine. As if I want this cruddy old house and a cruddy barn, that is next to it! In the back, there is a large red barn. It kind of reminds me of a cow barn. In any case, it is falling apart. An individual can hardly walk through it without feeling like something is going to fall on your head.

The boys and I are upstairs. I have a loft-style room and they are in a small room in the back of my room. I do not like it, but if I want a place to live I will have to endure this for now. I know Dad will not let me live here long. He has had his girlfriends coming and going. One I really do not like. She seems to think she runs this house. I have already had it out with her once. I am not sure how much longer I can take it. Dad likes to put everyone else above his family. That is one thing that is for sure.

So, for now, here we are. The nice thing about this house is that the elementary school is right around the corner. I can walk the boys to school. When the weather is junk I drive, but it is nice to be able to walk. When both of the boys are in elementary school I will be able to work more. As of right now, the weekend job is all I have. I do not like it as much but when the mall was sold, I lost my job there. New management. Ohh well!

I Miss You!

Love,
Ashley

Dear Mom, It's Me...

Today, I came home from my boyfriend's house. I was so pissed to see what had happened at the house. Dad had taken down all of your pictures. I was forced to clean the house to avoid his nonsense.

In the process of cleaning, I found the pictures shoved behind the couch. I am concerned about what is going to happen when he gets home. I am going to put them back up for now.

I went out on the back porch to smoke when his girlfriend came home. I asked her where my Dad was. She said he was on his way. I told her I needed to talk to him. She said, "What, you do not want to talk to me?" Satisfyingly, I told her no. I wanted to speak to my Dad. When he came home I asked him what this was all about. This was the only time that I really got into it with his girlfriend. She actually stood there and asked him if he was going to let me talk to her that way. I laughed because he just sat there with this "yeah" kind of look. In the end, I had to walk away. I did not want to escalate the issue any further.

I went upstairs and a few minutes later he came up with all the pictures. He threw them on my bed and walked back downstairs. The hardest part of this is that he still does whatever she says and does not listen to me. Same old Dad, different day. I had been spending less time at home and he had to have wondered why. Come on... This was the last straw. It was not long after this that I moved out. Well, he threw me out, but I still moved regardless. I can not take it any longer.

In the end, I am now living with my boyfriend and his two kids. We live in a small duplex. It is hard with the six of us, but we make do.

I Miss You!

Love,
Ashley

2005

Chapter 8

Dear Mom, It's Me...

It's been over a year since you passed away. Today was the worst day ever. I lost one of my best friends. I found out that Eric had gotten killed in a motorcycle accident. Even though he was wearing his helmet, it still cracked his head when he hit the tree. I got a phone call from someone we both know. He had asked me if I knew whether or tos true. I did not want to believe him. I was hoping that this was just a rumor. I ended up calling his parents and they told me. They said, yes it was true, and that they would keep me posted with the details.

After this phone call, I lost it. I think I cried as much, if not more when you passed. The hardest thing is that we kind of expected you to pass, but I never expected this.

I am not even sure how I am capable of understanding what happened. He was always there. Even though we had not talked in a while, I knew that no matter what I could always call him. He was like a big brother to me. I remember when he lived with us for a while. It was so nice to be able to see him whenever I wanted to. I enjoyed being able to sit downstairs with him while he read or flipped through a magazine.

The last time I saw him was after my oldest child was born. I had asked him to be his godfather. I was so happy when he accepted. I knew then, that my son would be taken care of if something happened.

It is so hard to have one loss right after another. It is not fair. Losing you was one thing, but losing Eric is quite another. I will say this much-having the boyfriend that I had at the time was a gift. He was so good to me and the boys. He made sure that I was ok and took care of the boys when I couldn't. Depression began to sink in. I know that this too shall pass, but seriously, how much more can one person take?

I Miss You!

Love,
Ashley

Dear Mom, It's Me...

I went to Eric's visitation today. It was very hard. His parents cremated him. I am sure that due to his injuries, they needed to. I do not think I would be able to see him in any other image. I prefer to remember him as he was. My boyfriend went with me and a friend was watching the kids.

I felt horrible because I had not really been much of a staple in his life after everything fell apart. I do not understand why this happened. We were all close friends. When I tried to introduce my boyfriend to his parents I accidentally mixed his mom with his sister. I am sure they understand. My mind was not really in the best place.

The visitation was beautiful. They had him in a nice urn with pictures of him all over the place. It is interesting to see him in a different light than what I had already known. He was a big brother to me in every way.

We did not stay long. There were not a lot of people there I knew, so I felt really out of place. It always seemed like Eric and I were in our little world. There were others we hung out with, but in the end, it was always just us. I did not see any of our other friends when we were there. I am not sure if they knew about it or not. I was only worried about making sure I was there. This has got to be one of the worst times in my life. I never expected to bury my mother, let alone say goodbye to my best friend. What is next?

I Miss You!

Love,
Ashley

Dear Mom, It's Me...

Today, we found out that your Dad is sick. He has colon cancer. Grandma seems to think that he will be ok. After everything that happened to you, it is hard to believe. Grandma said that he just needed to go to a specialist. Once he is there we will know more. He still looks really good. One would never know that anything was wrong with him.

A couple of days later Grandma told me that he had to have a colostomy bag. Not going to lie. It is kind of gross. I understand that it is for a good reason and he needs it for his health, but still. I feel bad for him. I hope that he is ok. I really do not think that I can watch this again. It was hard enough watching you go from being happy and healthy to nothing but skin and bones. The sunk-in parts of your face will haunt me forever.

I Miss You!

Love,
Ashley

Dear Mom, It's Me...

My boyfriend proposed to me!! I am getting married. Wow, I can not believe this. I knew it was going to happen, just was not sure when. We had been talking about rings and what I would want. I showed him a couple of different ones. He got the exact one that I asked for.

It was not that expensive, but it looked amazing. It is a princess-cut diamond with a row of diamonds under the cut. I really like it. I sent my sister a text message right after it happened. She is happy for me.

I just hope that once we are married we can get into a bigger place. There is not a lot of room here for all of us.

It is hard to even think about getting married when Grandpa is sick, plus not having you in my life, in addition to the fact that I have not talked to Dad in a couple of years now. I have no intention of inviting him. I really do not want the drama. However, it would be nice if I had an actual wedding. We shall see what time brings.

I Miss You!

Love,
Ashley

Dear Mom, It's Me...

Today, I went to visit Grandpa. He is not doing well at all. Hospice is there on and off. They make him comfortable and help keep him clean. I am glad they are there because this would be a lot to put on Grandma all the time. Every minute I am there, it reminds me of you. It is really hard. I cry a lot after each visit. It has been five years since you passed. It feels like it was just yesterday.

They say he does not have much more time. I worry about Grandma once Grandpa is gone. She will be in that big house all by herself. I know your sisters will be there often, but still. They have been together for decades. They have been married since 1949 and it is not even 2009 yet.

I hope that you and Grandpa will be able to find each other in heaven. I often wonder how big it is. When people die, everyone says they go to heaven. It must be a big place to fit all those people in it. Is it just a bunch of clouds with people floating on them? I wonder if little angels are flying around with big harps that play all day. I wish I could talk to you to understand what it is like there. I guess at some point I can only hope to join my friends and family. With all the trouble I have been in, I wonder if there is a place for me there. In the end, I will find out. If and when Grandpa does join you, please be sure to take care of him for me.

I Miss You!

Love,
Ashley

Dear Mom, It's Me...

I am sure you already know that Grandpa passed today. I think he was looking for you in heaven when he left us. He must have found you because now he is gone. He died in his home and peacefully went into a deep sleep. We were all there so grandma was not alone. I felt so bad for her. There was so much love there. They were such a cute couple.

His funeral will be in a couple of days. They have scheduled a visitation the day before. I am surprised that they could do this so quickly. I am sure with him being an army vet they will have the 21-gun salute, etc. He deserves that. These always scared me, though. They did the same thing at Grandpa K's funeral. Every time they fired, I jumped.

I do not understand why I am not that sad about Grandpa. I think it is because with his cancer it was expected. I think this is reflected in what I went through with you. After so much death it gets harder to cry, to be sad, and to express my feelings. I know grandma knows. Grandma has talked about why I found it difficult to go over there.

I Miss You!

Love,
Ashley

Dear Mom, It's Me...

The odd thing about life is how much we realize how we are like our parents. Every day, it gets more and more obvious that I am like both of you. You, for the fact that I am not afraid to work. Throughout my life, I have always worked. You know for a fact that I started working young. Over the course of a couple of years, I have worked two jobs for a year straight each. I can understand why you were always tired. It takes a lot out of you when you go from sun up to sun down. Especially when it is seven days a week. There is much to be said that I have your "badass" attitude. That is one thing that has not changed. Your sisters even agree; they see a lot of you in me.

I have also enjoyed your love for the water and being outside. The summertime is my favorite time of year. I love going out on the lake and enjoying the sun. We got a boat, and being out on it has become one of my favorite things to do. I like being able to lay out and go swimming. I am not a huge fan of being in the lake (would rather have a pool), but this is most definitely a less expensive way.

On the other hand, it appears as though I have picked up some of Dad's traits as well. The one thing that I noticed the most is the fact that I might be better off working for myself. I know Dad always did because he could not stand someone telling him what to do. I do not mind. Just the drama associated with working with other people is annoying. Another thing I noticed is smoking. I own up to the fact that this was also my choice, but at the same time, Dad always smoked around us kids. That is bound to rub off as well. I have seen it with my own kids. I can not blame them because it is what a mom does. However, I wish they would not have started.

Getting older, you realize that at some point we are going to be like our parents. All my life I told myself that I would never be like Dad or do the things he did. However, there is some part of me that knows I have those similarities. That bothers me. I do not mind having your traits, but at the same time, I worry. I guess we are in charge of our own destiny.

I Miss You!

Love,
Ashley

Chapter 9

Dear Mom, It's Me...

Today, I feel like I am the happiest woman in the world. I was working at the store and received a call for an interview. The coolest thing is that I was referred to this school. I am so excited. They are having me start at the end of August. That is two weeks away. I will be teaching 9th-grade English. It is a long-term substitute position, but I will take it. Even if they do not hire me permanently, who knows how long the actual teacher will be out? This is going to be an interesting transition from being a manager here to managing 9th graders. The only thing that continues to eat at me is that the school is in Grand Rapids. I did not expect to have to drive so far, but for now, I will take it.

I understand that this will be a once-in-a-lifetime opportunity, and I am not going to pass it up. I have worked so hard through school to get here. The principal who called me seems like a nice individual. The experience will also help me to boost my career as long as it goes well.

The whole Covid thing is still going on. I need to be prepared to begin this year through online platforms. I am familiar with some of this, but the question is, how am I supposed to keep these kids occupied that long on the internet? I guess we will see.

This will be a full-time. I will need to put my resignation in at my current work. At least I have the two-week's notice. I did warn the new store manager that this will happen. I hope that she will receive this information like an adult. I have my doubts. I did make sure to write out the resignation because I never know if I may need to come back. I think if I did, it would not be this store though. It really has become too much with her working here.

I Miss You!!

Love,
Ashley

Dear Mom, It's Me...

Well, I was right. She got the posted note on the wall. I just got home from work and got my usual phone call. Only this time, she is making a huge deal out of it. I told her that this would come. She called me to complain as much as she could. I told her that we had already talked about this when she first started. She got all butt hurt and decided to go through the district manager. She wanted to fire me, and that is what she did. Oh well. I know that where I am going I will be very happy and not have to work fifty-plus hours a week.

I feel bad though. I do not want to lose my customers who are also my friends. I am pretty confident that this place will go downhill once I am gone. In any case, there is no point in crying over spilled milk, right? I have to get my mind focused for the upcoming year.

I Miss You!

Love,
Ashley

Dear Mom, It's Me...

I am excited to say that I have started my new job at the school. I never in a million years thought, after all those years of hard work, I would be right where I wanted to be. We are starting the school year online due to COVID nonsense. It is hard to teach online. I never really know if they are doing their work or not. I don't have a turn-in system that works well. I have used document sharing in order to see what the kids are doing. That seems to work to a point. It is really nice that the kids are responding to me pretty quickly though.

I think the one thing I have learned is not to be their best friend and to be their teacher instead. I love how the kids are so willing to open up to me, but at the same time, I feel like they take advantage of me too. Sometimes being too kind can come back and bite you in the butt.

The kids are back at school now. Thank goodness. I love being able to see them regularly. I have a few that I could do without, but the rest. I am all for it.

I Miss You!

Love,
Ashley

Dear Mom, It's Me....

I have been teaching for a couple of months now. It has been great. I have had a few ups and downs, but nothing serious. I have one class in the morning that is just something else. The kids do not ever talk or do their homework. This is great most of the time. However, some days it would be nice to be able to build on that relationship with them. I can not say I do not have favorites in the classes, but they are all pretty great. We have been working our way through the book *Of Mice and Men*. I remember this book from when I was at Hamilton High School. My mentor teacher was awesome and gave me a bunch of stuff for teaching. I also found things in the room I could use. It is so nice to be able to say that I have my own classroom. I can do whatever I want to do with it.

With COVID-19, I have to have the kids all sit forward. I wish I did not have to do this. It would be easier to have them sit in a circle or in groups. I think as a teacher, it is easier to have the kids sit in groups. A group setting makes it easier to move people around if necessary.

I Miss You!

Love,
Ashley

Dear Mom, It's Me...

Today, I did something I probably shouldn't have. The kids in class were messing with their water bottles in class. I kind of coaxed a student to spray another student with water. This was a huge mistake. It ended up being an all-out water fight in class.

Aside from not being an adult in this case. There were a couple of computers that got soaked. Ooops, my bad! It wasn't so bad and really funny until the electronics got damaged. As I have mentioned before, it is really hard sometimes to know how to act.

I want to be their teacher and their friend at the same time. I give examples of things in my personal life that reflect on what we are doing. However, I question whether or not I should be sharing this information. Sometimes I feel like it makes my job easier if the kids know who I am and what I am all about. I want them to see me as a real person and not just another teacher they have to deal with. I guess we will see.

I Miss You!!

Love,
Ashley

Dear Mom, It's Me...

Today has been a weird day. My sister called me to say that Dad was in the hospital. Apparently, he has COVID-19 and it is pretty bad. I don't know, I have not talked to him in three years. My sister suggested I go to visit him, but I do not know how I feel about that. I understand he is sick and I should because you never know what will happen. At the same time, it would give me a chance to say the things I need to say.

Going to his room, I had to cover up like there was a toxic chemical spill. Everything has to be covered up from my head to my toes. It is nice that the nurse comes in with me to help me tie things and make sure nothing can get in. This reminds me of the movie *Outbreak*. Especially the part where they have to get all covered up to avoid the airborne illness. In a way, COVID-19 is the same due to the airborne part of it.

I ended up going to see him. He is on a breathing mask and coughs a lot. So, we try not to have him talk too much. As usual, when he sees me, he starts crying. I have never understood why he does that. He knows that he messed up with me as his daughter. These were all things that he chose to do and it was not me. I did everything he ever asked of me while living at home. I do not understand why he has to be such a jerk.

I Miss You!

Love,
Ashley

Dear Mom, It's Me...

Why is there so much drama with this man? My now ex-friend is trying to have my sister and I sneak a drug into the hospital for Dad. What is wrong with her? She needs to understand that this is illegal. Obviously, we are not going to do it. Now, I have to show an ID and have a password to get into the room. We have enough to deal with right now. This is not something that should be an issue.

In any case, I am glad I do not have to worry about her getting in. The last thing we need is for the hospital to think that it was one of us. I guess she sent a pretty nasty text message to my sister about it as well. I ended up texting her to tell her that if she or her Dad harassed us anymore, I would file harassment charges. I am glad that I am not friends with her any longer. In a way, it makes me sad, but in other ways, I am not worried about it. She totally lost me as a friend as the years went by. I have done some pretty nasty things, but there are just some things that she did that should not happen in life. Well, I'm safe for now. I guess.

I Miss You!!

Love,
Ashley

Dear Mom, It's Me...

Well, my sister and I had to make the decision today. Dad asked for it, but we ended up putting him on the ventilator. He was struggling to breathe even with the air mask. My sister called me and told me that I had to possibly come down to the hospital. She said they need us down there as a "just in case."

In the end, everything turned out fine. He is breathing with the machine now. They say he is not supposed to be on the ventilator too long. So, at this point, it just depends on whether or not his body will recover or not.

He seems to be doing pretty well, but the doctors are concerned about whether or not his organs will continue to function properly. I kind of wonder the same thing. With COVID-19, people are dying due to other illnesses in their bodies. I do not know of any with Dad (but then again, I have not been around him in three years.) I am guessing because he is overweight and a smoker there are risks. Who knows?

I Miss You!!

Love,
Ashley

Dear Mom, It's Me...

Dad has been on the ventilator for a couple of days now. I have stopped going to see him because he does not know I am even there. Plus, having to get all wrapped up to see him is kind of annoying. My sister goes to see him and fills me in on how he is doing. It helps some. I just do not want to go down there and see his stupid girlfriend. I will not be happy with that at all.

In any case, I am just working as much as I can right now. Trying to get money together for living life. I only wish I had it like you, where you made decent money and were able to still have a good time. I know that Dad never helped with any of that, but who knows?

Short write today. Everything is pretty much the same as the day before.

I Miss You!

Love,
Ashley

Dear Mom, It's Me...

My sister called today. It has been nearly a month with Dad on the Ventilator. The doctor said that there has not been any improvement in his condition. The only good thing is that the COVID-19 is gone. She asked me what my thoughts were. I am not sure why; she knows what they are already, but I respect her for it.

The doctors advised my sister that Dad's heart was starting to fail. Additionally, the other organs in his body are starting to shut down. We can see the difference in his heartbeat on the monitor. He is sweating a lot. The doctors say that it is because he has so much water in his body from lying down all the time. The nurse says that they roll him every once and a while, but it is not good for a human body to lie down all day long, every day.

My sister and I are talking about arrangements and such now. So, we will see what happens. Dad gave my sister power of attorney, so what happens is up to her.

I Miss You!

Love,
Ashley

Dear Mom, It's Me...

We made the decision today to pull Dad off the ventilator. His body is shutting down to the point that he will not recover. My sister arranged for all of us to come down to say goodbye at different times. It would have been horrible if I had been there when his "little thing" was there.

Auntie and I went down at the same time. I was not sure if I wanted to be in the room alone or with her. After all these years, what can I say to him? I am not even sure how I feel about him dying. Truthfully, I always hoped that, in the end, it would have been him over you, but we can't pick and choose like that.

The weird thing is he died on the exact date that you passed, 4:04 p.m. I am starting to think that this is going to be a family thing. I did not stay until the end. The waste bag was on my side of his bed and it stunk big time. Not to mention the hospital priest was hanging too close to me. I had to leave. I felt bad, but I was uncomfortable.

I Miss You!

Love,
Ashley

Chapter 10

Dear Mom, It's Me...

It is interesting how some individuals develop to become lifelong learners. I am not sure how this happens, especially when people like me didn't go to school in the past. Now, it seems as though I can not get enough of it.

I took my entire first Master's Degree online. Yep, Mom, that is right. I have obtained not only one but two Master's Degrees. My first is in Business/Human Resource Management. With the second, I had the insane notion of becoming a teacher. My second Master's I finished in Education/Instruction and Curriculum. I do not want to stop.

I love writing (as you know). I have been writing since I was a kid. I know that those stories were not always appropriate for someone my age, but I remember you telling me that you actually thought that they were good. Although, I do prefer those stories over writing ones that create an emotional nut-bag.

I do enjoy remembering all the good times that I had as a kid. Even, the times that were spent making up for lost time. I was not even sure that you could do that, but you managed to perfectly. In reality, some of the memories that came up with writing this also created even worse memories. I really wish that there was a chance that I could go back and do so much of my life over again. I do not have regrets. I wish I could make changes. Changes that would have improved my future, both as a parent and as an educated woman.

Guess what Mom? We never knew everything, even though most of my life was spent pretending I did. All I can hope for now is closure, peace, happiness, and to feel whole again.

I Miss You!!

Love,
Ashley

Dear Mom, It's Me...

I have also learned the love you shared with owning a Jeep. I now have two different Wranglers. I have always wanted one and it is amazing to own one. I was not happy when I found out that Dad sold yours. I know it was a stick, but I could have at least learned how to drive it. With one Wrangler, we did a complete off-the-frame restoration, and with the other, we are in the process of fixing it up. It is really exciting when people look at my purple Wrangler and tell me how nice it is. I enjoy saying thank you and seeing people's faces. We are going to paint the older one I got with a Jurassic Park theme. I love those movies and I remember watching them with you.

The thing about being married to a mechanic is that I can do all of these things and not have to pay someone to do it for me. My youngest has also learned a lot about fixing cars and such. He has also taken up the life of a mechanic. I am so proud of him. He is doing great things with his life, but he works way too much. He enjoys it though and that is all that matters.

I Miss You!

Love,
Ashley

Dear Mom, It's Me...

The hardest part about life is when everyone around you has either died or moved away. It makes you question what is left in life. I think for me the holidays are the worst. After Grandma got super sick, the family stopped getting together. I am so used to going to Grandma's on Christmas Eve and Grandpa K's house on Christmas morning. Those were always the best times. I know it has been years since we got together as a family, but it still bothers me. I often wonder if I can let go of my past and be able to move forward. I guess, as most would say, I am a damaged person. Maybe this is why my oldest son hates me.

He is doing everything that I did at his age. The hardest part is, I do not want him to go through life having regrets. I have discovered that it is not the best way to live your life. After you passed away, it really hit me hard. It continues to bother me, but at the same time, I understand that there is nothing I can do about it now. I can only move forward and try to fix any wrongs while making sure I do the right thing.

I Miss You!

Love,
Ashley

Dear Mom, It's Me...

I wanted to write this book/novella as a means of closure. It is really difficult when someone you love has left you so quickly. During your illness, there never felt like there was a good time to say anything. It felt like there was always someone around you. I do not know, maybe I am just making up excuses.

I just really want to say that I am sorry. I am sorry for my life choices that you were upset with me for. I think most of all, I am sorry for the way I treated you as a child. I know I was never that cooperative or obedient. I understand that it took me a long time to realize what was happening. It is hard to fathom that it took me having a child to grow up some.

I think most of all, I am sorry I was not there as often as I should have during your illness. I think it was really hard for me to comprehend what was happening. I did not want to lose my mother and be stuck with my dad. I appreciate everything you have/had done for me. I know it must have been a challenge to work two jobs and take care of the house.

I am not trying to write this novella looking for sympathy, sorrow, or to promote mental health. I wrote this not only for closure but also to let others understand that even though we may have difficult situations, some of which may border on devastating, we can always pull through. Remember, to never let go of your dreams. Allow your dreams to take you wherever you want to go.

So, dear reader, I challenge you to take one situation in your life and create closure, using whatever means you believe will help and motivate you. Always make sure to keep your head up and know that you are worthy and beautiful. This too shall pass.

I Miss You!!

Love,
Ashley

Dear Mom… It's Me… I Miss You!
By: Ashley Kammeraad Zuidema

Dear Mom, It's Me… I Miss You! is a novel written from a young girl's perspective. The girl explains events that have happened in her life, with a large focus on the loss of her mother. Just before turning twenty-one years old, she experiences what it is like to grow up without a mother. The author explains the difficulties that she had to go through while growing up. This heartwarming tale will have you at the edge of your seat with every page turn. This book is an outright page turner that keeps you guessing and wondering what will happen next.

Ashley is a published author. Her first book is through an anthology entitled "The Mindful Journey," which can be found on Amazon.

Ashley is a current Instructional Assistant at a local elementary school. She is a mother, grandmother, and an avid crafter. Ashley currently resides in Zeeland, MI.

Links:
Landing Page:
https://sherisesstudios-3777c.gr8.com/
Blog:
https://livingthedreamgettingpublished.blogspot.com/
Instagram: @ashleyzuidema

Synopsis

"She exists now, only in my memories." Kate Winslet

"Dear Mom, It's Me... I Miss You!" is a novel based on the author's personal life experiences. Through the use of letters, the author expresses her thoughts, feelings, and memories of her mother. When we lose someone, we generally feel as though we never got the chance to say what needed to be said. This is the author's chance to do so. This epistolary novel embraces the hurt that a daughter goes through when suffering the loss of their mother.

Darkness had fallen over the house. It was hard to stay positive in a situation where hope felt lost. Not knowing what was going to happen consumed the emptiness inside. There has never been a worse time in Ashley's life. The loss of her mother caused unbearable pain. A young adult should never have to go through seeing someone suffer, let alone someone close to them, like a parent. With the end being so close to her birthday, the author finds it harder and harder to find a way to move on. The hope with the publication of this book is that the author will be able to feel at peace.

As a young girl, being a daddy's girl would have been the best thing in the world. Yet, in Ashley's case, she was a momma's girl. Her mother worked two jobs to support the family, was a motorcycle enthusiast, and a sunbathing beauty queen. Ashley's mom was always busy or away. Yet, they made the best of the times they had together.

The chapters of this book are broken down into life phases. In the beginning, the author dives into her childhood and the happy times she had, sharing riveting memories of teenage adolescence and crazy friends. The middle descends into the tragic loss of her mother and how cancer opened her eyes to what it can do. Thereby realizing how precious life can be and how we need to value the ones we have and the time we have with them. The last section ends with the author telling us what her life has been like without her mother and how she has been handling it.

The author hopes that other readers will feel like they are not alone - to empower readers to come forward with their stories and feel good about telling them. There can be happiness in life when there is a loss. This novel may not be relatable to everyone, but there is someone out there who might just appreciate it.

About the Author

 Mother & Wife, Life-long learner, Educator, and Author. Ashley was born and raised in Holland, MI. Over the last 15 years, she has utilized her passion for education and learning, while obtaining two Master's degrees—one from Baker College in Business, and the other from Grand Valley State University in Education. Ashley enjoys reading, crafting/journal making, and her love for her animals. She is determined to be successful at whatever she does and takes pride in her hardworking nature.

Ashley is currently working as an Instructional Assistant at a local elementary school. She has attempted to take her Michigan Teachers Certification test multiple times and finds that she enjoys the ability to write and added freedom much more enjoyable. Ashley's mission is to empower women to take chances, fulfill their dreams, and understand there is so much more to life than we could have ever imagined.

www.ingramcontent.com/pod-product-compliance
Lightning Source LLC
Chambersburg PA
CBHW071025120626
46546CB00003B/1224

* 9 7 8 1 9 6 0 1 3 6 6 3 3 *